This book belongs to

....

The STORY of CHRISTMAS

First published in Great Britain in 2021

Society for Promoting Christian Knowledge
36 Causton Street, London SW1P 4ST
www.spck.org.uk

British Library Cataloguing-in-Publication Data
A catalogue record for this book is available from the British Library

ISBN 978-0-281-08404-3

Printed by Imago

Produced on paper from sustainable forests

The STORY of CHRISTMAS

Alexa Tewkesbury
Illustrated by Dani Padrón

spck

There is **light**. A dazzle of light all around.

But not from the sun. Not from the moon.

The light shines from the **angel Gabriel's** bright, beaming face.
'Mary!' says Gabriel.

'Who – me?' asks Mary. 'You don't mean **me**?'

'Yes, you!' says Gabriel. 'I have something wonderful to tell you. Listen!'

Mary listens. Mary stares.

'**God** is **sending his Son** into the world,' Gabriel says. 'He'll be born here as a tiny baby. He'll show everyone how much God loves them. And God wants you to be his **mother**, Mary. You! You're to call him **Jesus**.'

Mary stares even more. 'Oh my!' she says.

There's a flurry. A soft flurry of air.

But not from a breeze. Not from a breath.

It's the flurry of an angel's wings.

'**Joseph!**' whispers the angel.

'Who – me?' asks Joseph. 'You don't mean **me**?'

'Yes, you!' says the angel. 'Take Mary to be your wife.
Then you can both bring up God's Son **together**.
It's what God **wants** you to do.'

Joseph's eyes open wide. 'Oh my!' he says.

Weeks pass. Then months.

Until it's almost time for Mary to have her baby.

But the **emperor** says, 'How big is my empire? How many people live here? Everyone must go to their home town to be **counted**!'

'Who – us?' asks Mary. 'The emperor doesn't mean **us**?'

'Yes, us,' says Joseph. 'Everyone. We must go to **Bethlehem**.'

What a **long** journey!

And Bethlehem town is busy. When Mary and Joseph arrive, there is **nowhere** for them to stay.

Mary is tired. She needs a warm, quiet place to have her baby.

An innkeeper says, 'There are people staying in all the rooms at my inn, but I do have a **stable** for my animals. If you like, you can rest there.'

'Must I have my baby in a stable?' wonders Mary. 'Oh my!' she says.

There are tears. Teardrops on Mary's face.
But not from sadness. Not from fear.
These are happy tears.

Jesus, **God's Son,** has been **born**. Mary lays straw in the animals' feeding tray. A bed for her baby boy.

On a hilltop above the town,
shepherds watch over
their sheep.

But what's that – that gleam of light
through the darkness . . . ?

Even the sheep look surprised.

Another angel in the night sky!
God's angels are busy.

‘Don’t be scared,’ says the angel. ‘God’s Son has been born in Bethlehem. A **king,** to bring **peace and joy** to the world. Go – find him!’

‘Who – us?’ ask the shepherds. ‘You don’t mean **us**?’

‘Yes, you!’ says the angel. ‘**God** wants you to be the first people to visit him.’

All at once comes the sound of **singing**. Louder and louder.

The sky is full of **angels,** all **singing** to God!

The shepherds laugh and run away to meet Jesus.
'Oh my!' they say.

There's a twinkle far away. A twinkle in the night.

But not from a lantern. Not from a flame.

It's the twinkle of a star with **good news** to tell.

‘We must follow this star where it takes us,’ say some **wise men**. ‘It brings news of a young king!’

The star leads them on and on . . .
All the way to **Jesus**.

In front of Jesus, the wise men **kneel down**.

They give him presents. **Gold** and **frankincense** and **myrrh**.
Gifts for a king – the most **special king** who has ever been born.

'This is God's own beautiful boy,'
Mary thinks to herself.
'Oh my!' she says.

How many angels
did you spot?

How many animals did you spot?

Noah and His Ark

978-0-281-07496-9

Daniel in the Lions' Den

978-0-281-07498-3

Jonah and the Whale

978-0-281-07500-3

The Story of Easter

978-0-281-08395-4

spck